Vital Faith

Practical, wise advice for living

an in-depth devotional study
of the book of James

GREG GRIFFIN

To my family and to God's glory

Introduction

Welcome to this exciting adventure called *Vital Faith*. Over the next 43 days, you'll read through the book of James in small, tidbits—just a few verses a day. Even though you could read lots more each day, do your best to read just one day's reading at a time. It might be tempting to read through this manual like a novel, just taking in the information in a passive manner. But hold on, because James's style is clear, direct, and to the point. It will shake you and wake you. The theology here isn't super deep, but it is a super-solid application of the gospel of Jesus Christ in simple, easy-to-understand language.

I encourage you to read the day's verses and then reflect on what God has for you in His truth. Chew on it, stew on it, pray over it. Write any thoughts or questions. You might even journal a few reflections each day. Let this manual become a working tool to grow you more into the person God designed and desires you to be. I also encourage you to find a friend or two who will take this journey with you, and meet once a week to share with one another, stretch one another, and support one another.

For James, faith isn't something to debate or just discuss — it's for everyday life and use. Talk is cheap. Just do it. My goal in this manual is for us to gain or keep a vital faith that directs us from the inside out and carries us when life gets hard, so we can "just do it," plain and simple.

Vital Faith. If it's vital, it will be visible. That's my prayer for each one of us who takes on this study.

Because of Jesus,

Greg Griffin

DAY 1

This letter is from James, a slave of God and of the Lord Jesus Christ. I am writing to the "twelve tribes"—Jewish believers scattered abroad. Greetings!   *James 1:1*

So who is this guy James? What gives him the authority to write this letter? Why was it important enough to be included in the Bible? Well, it turns out he's the earthly brother of Jesus. Not too shabby of a credential. We can read a little about him in the book of Acts. It's clear he's a leader of the early church that began after Jesus ascended into heaven. His letter (or, as we call it, book of the Bible) was probably one of the first Christian writings, written around AD 50. (Jesus died around AD 33.)

Scholars think James was pretty well known because he didn't feel the need to introduce himself as the Lord's brother. Instead, he calls himself a slave. Wow! What a different perception. That means he saw himself as an obedient, humble, and loyal follower. How'd you like to have your brother or sister refer to themselves like that when speaking about you? The Greek word for slave is *doulos*, the same word used to refer to Moses, Joshua and Caleb, Abraham, Isaac, Jacob, Job,

Isaiah, and other prophets.[1] By taking on the title *doulos,* James identifies himself with the great servants of history.

It is tough to be a Christian these days, but it was even tougher back then. It was lots more likely you could lose your life for being a follower of Jesus. A guy named Stephen was stoned to death, and after that Christians scattered from Jerusalem, all over the Roman world. They didn't have a First Community Church to go to in their city, so James wrote to the scattered followers as a concerned leader, to encourage them in their faith during those difficult times.

Things haven't changed much, have they? It's still hard to live as a Christian. We're not yet persecuted with the threat of death here in America, but we're definitely in a post-Christian world that makes it hard to live out our faith. Let's see what James has to say for us in the coming weeks.

—————— **So what?** ——————

1.   What would it have been like to be the brother or sister of Jesus?

2.   How do you think it would feel to be disconnected from other Christians when this was written, and then get a copy of James's letter?

3.   Would you call yourself a slave of Christ? Why or why not?

———————— **Prayer** ————————

God, help me be open to Your truth as I read Your Word in this study. Amen.

—— **More words from the Word** ——

Acts 12:17
Acts 15:13
Acts 7:55–8:3

DAY 2

Dear brothers and sisters, when troubles come your way, consider it an opportunity for great joy. For you know that when your faith is tested, your endurance has a chance to grow. So let it grow, for when your endurance is fully developed, you will be perfect and complete, needing nothing.   *James 1:2–4*

Talk about an abrupt transition. James says in verse one, "Hi, it's me, James. How are you?" Then, boom. He gets right to it, and in a surprising way. He says we should let our troubles be opportunities for joy. That's not what usually pops into my mind when trouble finds me. But we have to admit James makes a truthful point about growth. Faith is like a muscle. The more you use it, the stronger it gets. That's just the way it is, and there's no shortcut, because a shortcut would cut our faith short of what it can and needs to be. Our faith in Christ grows stronger under *pressure*, not under pleasure.

James uses a word for *test* that is used to refer to the purification of metal. The goal of testing, James says, is to make us pure. So a faith test is an *opportunity for purification*, a spiritual workout that grows our faith to make us stronger.

An athlete works hard, not so he will collapse, but so he will develop more strength and staying power. In this world, trouble spots are not meant to take the strength out of us but to put the strength into us. To put it another way, a test is given to see if a student can pass, not pass out. You've heard it said that adversity builds character. That's true. It's also true that adversity *reveals* character.

So what?

1. Looking back, how has God given you strength to face a difficult situation in your past?

2. How has your relationship with God changed as you have gone through trials and difficulties?

3. What's going on in your life right now that's an opportunity to let your endurance grow?

Prayer

God, help me to see whatever happens today as something you can use to help me grow. Amen.

—— More words from the Word ——

Acts 5:41
2 Peter 1:6
Romans 5:3–5

DAY 3

> If you need wisdom, ask our generous God, and he will give it to you. He will not rebuke you for asking. But when you ask him, be sure that your faith is in God alone. Do not waver, for a person with divided loyalty is as unsettled as a wave of the sea that is blown and tossed by the wind. Such people should not expect to receive anything from the Lord. Their loyalty is divided between God and the world, and they are unstable in everything they do.
>
> *James 1:5-8*

Ah, wisdom. It's the commodity of kings. It would be hard to find someone who doesn't see wisdom as a good thing. And James says he "knows a guy," where you can get wisdom if you need it. And this wisdom isn't some cheap, discounted stuff, but the best of the best, straight from the God of the entire universe! The word James uses for wisdom isn't really translated "knowledge," which might be our first thought; it's discernment and decision-making skills. James knew many people that had lots of information in their heads, and, as we say, had a lot of "book sense." Common sense is what James is referring to in verse 5, a practical wisdom that's needed when you face tough choices. That's why James jumps from talking about withstanding troubles (yesterday's reading) to wisdom, because they are connected. We'll need wisdom to see how to these are opportunities and not obstacles.

James has the solution: ask God. God will gladly tell you. Any parent can relate. If your child asked you for help making a wise choice, you'd do a back flip (especially if he's a teenager!). God will help us out by granting us direction in our decision-making. So, if you ask, don't doubt. *The only reason one would waffle when asking God for wisdom is if that person isn't sure God's ways are best.* James says God wants us to trust Him fully, or don't bother. Trust Him. Fully. Or don't bother. So be bold, not because of who you are but because of who God is! Ask Him, and God will gladly give you wisdom for what you're facing.

—————— So what? ——————

1. What keeps you from asking God for wisdom?

2. When is a time when you didn't ask God for wisdom in a tough situation and later wished you had?

3. What are some ways God "tells" you when you ask? In other words, how will you recognize God's answers?

───── Prayer ─────

God, You said I could ask for more wisdom, so I'm asking. Give me more wisdom. Let me keep the truth of Your sovereignty *and* righteousness *in the front of my mind, so I won't doubt Your instruction. Amen.*

── More words from the Word ──

1 Kings 3:9
Job 23:10
Proverbs 2:3–6
Matthew 7:7

DAY 4

Believers who are poor have something to boast about, for God has honored them. And those who are rich should boast that God has humbled them. They will fade away like a little flower in the field. The hot sun rises and the grass withers; the little flower droops and falls, and its beauty fades away. In the same way, the rich will fade away with all of their achievements.

James 1:9–11

God uses every situation to give people just what they need. James teaches us that God gives poor people a special honor, because they are able to see more clearly that the most important things in life aren't things. And wealthy people receive a special insight on humility, because they learn very quickly that money can be here today and gone tomorrow. James says the poor should be glad that riches mean nothing to God; otherwise they might consider themselves unworthy. The rich should be glad that money means nothing to God, because money is easily lost.[1]

Our society puts so much value on money and having a bunch of comforting stuff. The follower of Jesus has to find a way to see past those things, to the real value God has on our lives. It's *all* about the heart. The poor can see that truth because their lives aren't filled with distractions. The wealthy can see that only when they realize that a life dependent on riches and acquisitions is very shaky at best. And at some point in life, every person has to come to grips with the fact that their hearse won't be outfitted with a hitch for a U-Haul trailer.

———— So what? ————

1. If I lost all my material goods in a fire or a hurricane, what would be left?

2. How has my experience with possessions or lack of them shaped my faith?

3. How can I fight back against society's value system?

———— Prayer ————

God, teach me honor from my needs and humility from my excess. Amen.

—— More words from the Word ——

Job 14:2
Psalm 102:4, 11
Isaiah 40:6–7
1 Peter 1:24

DAY 5

God blesses those who patiently endure testing and temptation. Afterward they will receive the crown of life that God has promised to those who love him. *James 1:12*

Impatience is a weakness for most of us in the fast-paced part of the world we live in. We don't like it when we have to be patient, and we don't usually appreciate "opportunities" to grow our patience. And we cringe at the thought of being patient while going through a tough stretch. It's awfully hard to remember that God doesn't wear a watch. *We* live in a time dimension, but God doesn't. That's why we get impatient, because we're trying to fit God in on our clock.

When are you most likely to feel impatient? Probably when the going is tough. "Let's get past this! I want to be done with it!" James says when we instead endure the tough times with a patient spirit, leaning on God's timing instead of our own, we're like a metal that's being purified. It's a fact of science that pure metals are stronger than contaminated ores. The finest steel gets sent through the hottest furnace, and we are like metals. It's hanging tough during these times that brings a reward for the hope that we've held onto. It's the crown of life. That phrase means *the crown that consists of life*. The crown of the Christian is a new kind of living that is not just life, it's life indeed. Because of Jesus, we enter into a life even more abundant than we've known.

Did you know that God has a bunch of blessings He's just waiting to give you? Some are there for the asking; some are there as a result of trusting in God's ways during tough times when your patience is challenged.

Have you heard about the legend of the amazing Chinese bamboo tree? When the seed for this tree is planted, nothing is seen for *four years*, except for a small shoot coming from a small bulb. During this time, though, all the growth is underground, in a massive root structure than spreads deep and wide. In the fifth year, the Chinese bamboo tree grows up to *eighty* feet![1]

Be patient. God is at work in your life, even in tough times (*especially* in the tough times), building and preparing you for His work in His due time. And you *will* be rewarded, in this life and the next.

So what?

1. What kind of test is most likely to push your patience?

2. Is there a time you blew the chance to reap a blessing by being impatient for

God to show up or act on your timetable? What did you learn for the next challenge?

3. Who do you admire for their patience and resiliency? Ask them for pointers!

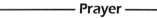

—————— **Prayer** ——————

God, remind me when I'm about to get impatient in a trial to look to You for perspective and peace. Amen.

—— **More words from the Word** ——

Job 5:17
Luke 6:22
Hebrews 10:36
Matthew 10:22

DAY 6

And remember, when you are being tempted, do not say, "God is tempting me." God is never tempted to do wrong, and he never tempts anyone else. Temptation comes from our own desires, which entice us and drag us away. These desires give birth to sinful actions. And when sin is allowed to grow, it gives birth to death. So don't be misled, my dear brothers and sisters.

James 1:13–16

Years ago, there was a hilarious comedian named Flip Wilson, and one of Flip's recurring characters was a woman named Geraldine whose frequent line was, "The devil made me do it." Well, that theology is almost spot on. You may have heard people say God was tempting them, but it's just not true. We've already learned in this study that God allows tests to make us stronger, just like a coach or teacher provides resistance to improve your performance. But when it comes to temptation, it's all about our weakness in resisting the devil. When we give in, it's bad news that doesn't seem so bad at the start, but it gets worse. Here's how verse 15 reads in Eugene Peterson's paraphrase Bible, *The Message*: "*Lust gets pregnant, and has a baby: sin! Sin grows up to adulthood, and becomes a real killer."* Ouch! Let's be clear. It's not a sin to be tempted. We will get bombarded with temptation all day, every day. The sin comes when we give way, and then it gets out of control.

Frogs have an interesting biological system. Their body temperature fluctuates to match the temperature of their surroundings. So, if you were to put a frog in a pot on a stove, and begin to heat the water, the frog's body temperature would slowly rise as the water's temperature rose. By the time the water boiled, the frog would literally be cooked to death, because he didn't jump out of the pot to save himself when the water got too hot. Sin can be like that—it grows ever so slowly that we don't realize the danger it places us in.

How many sports fans know who Michael Jordan is? But how many people know who Dickey Simpkins is? Both were members of the NBA champion Chicago Bulls when they won yet another championship in 1996–97. Simpkins averaged only 8 minutes of playing time and 1.9 points per game. You never heard a sportscaster say, "Well, Bill, the key to beating the Bulls is finding a way to stop Simpkins." He wasn't a threat! If you're not a threat, Satan doesn't need to worry about you.

So consider temptation a compliment. And then quickly as you can, turn your thoughts to God and the things of God to keep Satan away.

─────────── **So what?** ───────────

1. What is your Achilles' heel? Where is Satan most likely to attack you?

2. What is your plan of defense for the next attack? How can you be more ready to resist?

3. What signs will you look for to tell you to "jump out of the pot"?

─────────── **Prayer** ───────────

God, please help me to accept responsibility for my sins, and not blame you or someone else for my falling prey to temptation. Give me the presence of mind to break away from the temptation thought so it will die off, and to fix my thoughts on You and your Kingdom. Amen.

─── **More words from the Word** ───

Psalm 7:14
Isaiah 59:4
Romans 5:12; 6:23
1 Corinthians 10:13

DAY 7

> Whatever is good and perfect comes down to us from God our Father, who created all the lights in the heavens. He never changes or casts a shifting shadow. He chose to give birth to us by giving us his true word. And we, out of all creation, became his prized possession.   *James 1:17–18*

Wow! What a refreshing change from the doom and gloom of yesterday's portion of Scripture. That's because today's focus is God, not the Evil One. We learned yesterday that Satan's ways lead to death. Today's truth points to all the good and perfect stuff that comes from God. James says that we can rest on the fact that God and His good gifts will *never* change. Even though the heavenly lights God has made bring shadows as the sun moves, and the moon wanes and waxes, the God who made those lights is unchangeable. His Word is true and also unchangeable. What God says He will do, He will do. And He has chosen *us* to be His own children. What a mind-blowing thought! He loves you and me that much.

When you go to a fruit stand right when it opens first thing in the morning, you expect to see the really good stuff, the best of the best. That's why you go at that hour of the morning. You know from experience that if you go later in the day, the fruit that remains has been picked over. God talks about us as His children like that first and best fruit, and He has chosen us for Himself. God calls us His "choice possession" out of all creation, James says, and He bought us with the best gift of all of His good gifts, the gift of salvation through His Son Jesus. So, the next time you're feeling like you're not much, reread this verse to remind you that God claims *you* as his choice possession.

So what?

1.   What specific good gift does God provide to help you overcome your temptation?

2.   How can you remind yourself more often of God's goodness?

Prayer

Lord God, thank You for being the Giver of every good and perfect gift, especially for the gift of Jesus on the cross to offer me salvation. Give me eyes and ears and a heart to see Your goodness everywhere I turn today. Amen.

—— **More words from the Word** ——

Psalm 27:1
John 1:13
John 3:27
2 Corinthians 6:7
Hebrews 13:8

DAY 8

Understand this, my dear brothers and sisters: You must all be quick to listen, slow to speak, and slow to get angry. Human anger does not produce the righteousness God desires. *James 1:19–20*

Funny, most of us probably reverse each of these instructions. We're slow to listen, quick to speak, and quick to get angry. So how can we get it right?

Quick to listen

I think most of us would admit that often we're poor listeners. We either pretend we're listening while we're thinking about something else (or paying attention to our device), or we're busy thinking of what we're going to say in response when it's our turn. Just hearing isn't listening. I'm hearing impaired, and when I finally got a hearing aid, I told my friends, "Just because I can hear you better doesn't mean I can listen better."

The most basic, effective communication skill begins with a listening ear. If we're going to show people we value them, we must do what it takes to "be quick to listen." I like what the wise Steven Covey says: "Seek first to understand; then seek to be understood."[1]

Slow to speak

We're usually quick to speak because we feel the need to state or defend our position. My softball umpiring experience from years ago taught me that most people's frustration toward us is misdirected. Too often, we just happen to be in the line of their fire. If you react by speaking too quickly, it's not usually your best effort, and it often only makes a bad situation worse. In most every case, you can always say your mouthful later. Chances are if after reflection, you still feel the need to say it, you'll say it in a much more helpful manner. While you're thinking it over, a bigger perspective can prevail. We can ask ourselves what we need to say and why. Like toothpaste out of the tube, once our words are out, it's awfully hard to put them back in again. Speaking is one area of life when it's best to be slow. Our careful response can shine the light of Jesus in a big way.

Slow to get angry

James isn't writing about a righteous anger that lashes back at injustice, like the kind Jesus displayed when he knocked over the moneychangers' tables outside the Temple. James is talking about a *self*-righteous anger; we blow up because we just don't like something. What James is teaching us here is *macrothumos*, a Greek word that means "slow to boil." That's a good way to remember this truth, because "anger" is only one letter short of "danger."

───────── **So what?** ─────────

1. Which of these three directives speaks to your biggest weakness?

2. How can you be a better listener, and who needs you to listen most?

3. How will you remind yourself to resist speaking quickly?

4. In what area of your life do you need to be "slow to boil"?

───────── **Prayer** ─────────

God, please help me see how I can be a better listener, communicator, and in-control friend to those closest to me. Amen.

───── **More words from the Word** ─────

Proverbs 10:14; 12:18; 14:17
Matthew 21:12–17
Mark 11:15–19
Luke 19:45–48
John 2:13–16
Ephesians 4:26

DAY 9

> So get rid of all the filth and evil in your lives, and humbly accept the word God has planted in your hearts, for it has the power to save your souls. *James 1:21*

My mom loved to tell the story about the time she found me as a three-year-old, playing in the cold fireplace ashes in our home. She grabbed me by the wrists, and shook my little coal-black hands in front of my face, and said, "Just look at your hands! Just *look* at your hands!" I began to bawl, because I was mortified at how filthy I was, and I had no idea. I was oblivious.

James is doing a similar thing with his readers. "Just look at your lives! Get rid of the filth and evil." James tells us to shed the bad stuff we've gotten into, the way a snake sheds its skin. Strip it away. He uses strong words that communicate that immoral, deep-down dirt is causing spiritual ruin in many people. Before you can move on to wholeness, you will need to get rid of the filth and evil.

Then, James teaches us, accept what God has planted in you, with a teachable spirit. Put aside any cocky thoughts that you have it all together, he says, and open up your heart to receive the good gift of the good news. I'll bet James is remembering his brother Jesus's story about the Sower, which tells how the seed of the Word is sown into the hearts of men. He may also be referring to the conscience God created in every human that tells us right from wrong. God put that message in you with a voice that speaks from the inside, complementing His voice that speaks from the outside through his Word.[1] And that message is so vital because it is the message that brings eternal life.

So what?

1.   How clean are you? What do you need to rid yourself of?

2.   What's the condition of your "spirit soil" right now? Do you have a hard heart to God's Word, do you have lots of weeds that choke out the good, or are you too shallow to grow deep root, or are you fertile soil for God to do His good work in you?

3.   On a scale of 1 to 10, how would you rate your humility? What can you do to become more humble?

Prayer

Search me, O God, and know my heart; test me and know my thoughts. Point out anything in me that offends you, and lead me

along the path of everlasting life. Amen.
(Psalm 139:23–24)

—— **More words from the Word** ——

Matthew 13:1–8
Colossians 3:8

DAY 10

> But don't just listen to God's word. You must do what it says. Otherwise, you are only fooling yourselves. For if you listen to the word and don't obey, it is like glancing at your face in a mirror. You see yourself, walk away, and forget what you look like.
>
> *James 1:22–24*

Textbooks, websites, and YouTube videos are great—they can teach us how to do most anything by showing us diagrams, explaining things in detail, and giving step-by-step instructions. They can do most anything—except do it for us. We can read and study how to fly a plane, but that doesn't mean we can fly one. We can watch videos on how to kick a soccer ball, but that doesn't mean we can kick one. The same is true of our Christianity. Just because we read it in the Bible or hear about it in a message or small-group setting doesn't mean we can do it. We have to *apply* what we are learning as we actively put our faith into practice.

James says all listening and no doing is pretty foolish. Eugene Peterson's paraphrase in *The Message* is great: *"Don't fool yourself into thinking that you are a listener when you are anything but, letting the*

Word go in one ear and out the other. Act on what you hear!"

God uses the Bible to point out the areas we need to change in our lives. His Word brings knowledge about what needs to be changed, like a looking in a mirror and seeing a dirt smudge on your face. The mirror just shows where the dirt is, but it can't remove the dirt. (Did you ever see someone rub his or her face in the mirror to clean the smudge?) In order to remove the dirt, you'll need to get a cloth and maybe some water, and *apply* them to your smudge.

That's what can be dangerous about going to church or small group. You can go and hear somebody else talk about God, talk about growth, and leave thinking that somehow you've grown spiritually. The truth is you've just heard somebody else talk about it. Until *you* do something about it, you haven't really grown or made any progress spiritually. You just might be a little more knowledgeable, that's all.

——————— So what? ———————

1.   What smudge marks in your spiritual life are you aware of right now?

2.   Where have you just listened and stopped short of taking action to obey?

3.   What is holding you back from being obedient?

 Prayer

God, please help me to see the foolishness in my life where I know what is right, but I'm not obeying Your will. Help me to remember that Your way is what will bring me the most joy and peace, and that's why you command me to follow it. Amen.

More words from the Word

Matthew 7:21–28
Luke 6:46–49
Romans 2:13

DAY 11

But if you look carefully into the perfect law that sets you free, and if you do what it says and don't forget what you heard, then God will bless you for doing it. *James 1:25*

I love watching the different *CSI:* and other crime shows. Those detectives can find clues to solve a mystery where you think there are no clues. That's because they do the same kind of investigative work James suggests we do with God's law. The Greek word *parakypsas* ("looking steadily into") literally means "to stoop down" in order to have a good, close look. Take a good, close look at God's perfect law, James says. Don't just glance over it. Imagine how poorly CSI investigators would do their job if they just came to a crime scene, and after a quick look around shrugged their shoulders and looked at one another and said, "Beats me. Oh well."

The blessing for the detective, and for the follower of God's law, comes from taking the good, close look. That's where the payoff is. For the Jesus follower who does that, and acts on the law, the payoff is blessings from the hand of God, because he did what God instructed. He didn't miss the blessings because he just listened and then walked away.

James makes a point to say God's perfect law is the "law that sets you free." That sounds like a paradox, doesn't it? We tend to think of laws as restrictive, like a "can't do" list. That doesn't much sound like freedom. God's laws aren't as much restrictive (though they keep us from danger for sure) as they are directional. We should think of them as green lights to what God knows we really desire and need in this life, instead of red lights that prevent us from going where *we* think the fun is. In fact, when God says, "Thou shalt not," He's really shouting, "WRONG WAY! DANGER!" God's law is perfect, because it leads us to abundant life. The law is there to direct us to a fulfilled, free life. Would we expect anything less from a God who loves us enough to send Jesus to die for our sins so we can find our way to be with Him forever?

—————— So what? ——————

1.   How intently do you usually look at Scripture?

2.   Do you see God's direction as an overbearing parent who wants to control you, or do you see God as a loving parent who points out the danger spots to make your decisions less painful?

—————————— **Prayer** ——————————

God, give me eyes to see the deeper truth in Your Word that comes from a closer look. Help me commit your truth to memory so I won't forget it. Teach me ways I can hold on to Your truth. Write Your law on my heart. Amen.

——— **More words from the Word** ———

John 8:31–32
Romans 8:32
1 Peter 2:16

DAY 12

If you claim to be religious but don't control your tongue, you are fooling yourself, and your religion is worthless.

James 1:26

Years ago when our kids were small, I was driving my family home from a dinner out, and I noticed the car behind me was following too close for my comfort. I checked my speedometer, and I was going right at the speed limit. The other driver couldn't go around me because there was only one lane going in our direction, so he proceeded to "push" me by staying on my bumper. For some reason, it really got to me. And when he flashed his headlights at me to speed up, I did just the opposite. I slammed on the brakes momentarily to "communicate" back to him. That move about jerked my family out of their seats, and it caused the gentleman behind me to begin a new communication channel—sign language!

When we got to a red light, he pulled up in the available lane beside me, and I was ready, and he was too. I even had my window down. I didn't curse at him, but I'm not proud of what I said. As he pulled away, I was still steaming, and it wasn't like I could call out to invite him to worship with us one Sunday real soon.

From my counseling practice I've learned I'm not the only one who has a problem controlling the tongue. I'm sure you've heard someone who either professes to be a Jesus follower, or you know to be a Jesus follower, say something that made you wince as a fellow believer, because it's probably not what Jesus would do. Maybe they used some foul language. Maybe they gossiped. Maybe they weren't slow to boil, like me in the car that night, and they spewed all over someone else. James says that kind of person is just full of hot air. Wow — he gives us a tongue lashing with this teaching. Simply put, the authentic follower needs to control his or her tongue to be a true representative of Jesus. Here's a suggestion for us all: bite your tongue more often. That physical pain will go away a lot quicker than the pain you may inflict with ill-conceived conversation, and Jesus won't look bad to a world that needs to know Him.

————— So what? —————

1. When do you find that it's hardest to stay in control of your tongue?

2. Ask someone who loves you enough to tell you the truth how you can reduce the damage your tongue can create.

———————— Prayer ————————

*Lord God, please help me bite my tongue
to keep me from misrepresenting You. Amen.*

—— More words from the Word ——

Psalm 34:13

DAY 13

Pure and genuine religion in the sight of God the Father means caring for orphans and widows in their distress and refusing to let the world corrupt you.   *James 1:27*

There's a great story about a prominent American journalist some years ago doing a story on location in Calcutta about Mother Teresa's ministry to the lepers there. After watching Mother Teresa wash, caress, and care for these social outcasts, the journalist told Mother Teresa, "I wouldn't do what you do for a million dollars." Mother Teresa didn't miss a beat with her reply: "Neither would I."

James says, now that's religion. The orphans and widows were among the poorest of the poor in his day, and ministering to their needs is what we must do if we're Christ followers. This isn't a definition of religion, but a description of what true faith looks like. James says religion isn't a bunch of nice looking rituals, elaborate vestments, magnificent music, or a carefully planned worship service. It's doing something to relieve suffering in the name of Jesus. A friend of mine tells me about a church here in Atlanta where I live that has a sign you see as you exit the parking lot which reads:

"You are now entering the mission field." So "church" is what you do *after* you exit the building. Hmmm.

James also says true religion is a refusal to let the world corrupt you as a believer. The phrase he uses is better translated "keep yourself spotless" This is a directly opposite image of what he speaks about in verse 21 (Day 9), the moral filth we need to strip away from our lives. So that means we pay attention to our conduct to be sure it's not conformity to the world. Our hearts need to be doing what Jesus would do.

When you read about Jesus in the gospels, you read that Jesus always rooted for the underdog people that society wanted to ignore — the powerless, the poor, the left behind, the imprisoned, the orphaned, the widowed, the aged, the mentally ill, the social outcasts, sick, and the lepers. If Jesus was alive today, do you know who He would be hanging out with? Chronically ill and dying patients. He'd probably be at a hospice caring for those whom everybody else wants to kind of turn their back on. James would say, "Preach it, bro!"

We *must* be caring in order to be authentic followers.

─────────── **So what?** ───────────

1.   How easy or hard is it for you to get involved with someone who's the poorest of the poor?

2.   What steps can you take to make your religion pure and spotless, today?

3.   What can you learn from those you serve?

─────────── **Prayer** ───────────

Lord, please help me remember that when I serve the "least of these," I'm serving You. Move my heart to serve You more in this way. Amen.

─────── **More words from the Word** ───────

Isaiah 1:17
Matthew 25:34–36
Romans 12:2
1 Timothy 6:14
2 Peter 3:14

DAY 14

My dear brothers and sisters, how can you claim to have faith in our glorious Lord Jesus Christ if you favor some people over others? For example, suppose someone comes into your meeting dressed in fancy clothes and expensive jewelry, and another comes in who is poor and dressed in dirty clothes. If you give special attention and a good seat to the rich person, but you say to the poor one, "You can stand over there, or else sit on the floor"—well, doesn't this discrimination show that your judgments are guided by evil motives? Listen to me, dear brothers and sisters. Hasn't God chosen the poor in this world to be rich in faith? Aren't they the ones who will inherit the Kingdom he promised to those who love him? But you dishonor the poor! Isn't it the rich who oppress you and drag you into court? Aren't they the ones who slander Jesus Christ, whose noble name you bear? Yes indeed, it is good when you obey the royal law as found in the Scriptures: "Love your neighbor as yourself." But if you favor some people over others, you are committing a sin. You are guilty of breaking the law. *James 2:1–9*

Wise ol' Abraham Lincoln once said, "God must love the common people because he made so many of them." That was true then, it was true for James, and it's true now. James certainly was writing to correct a problem that was already there in the early church. Think about it. If you were a slave, or if you were at the bottom of the social ladder, Jesus offered you so much, while He demanded so much more from the rich. The church was full of those common people who embraced the good news of salvation and better life.

James's message is sharp: NO favoritism allowed. We are *all* God's children. There is no room for discriminating snobbery in God's church — End. Of. Discussion. He punctuates this teaching by saying if you treat the only rich with the "love thy neighbor" thing, you have broken the very law you use to justify your actions.

I remember my boss in a church I once served making me reduce the requirements for an exciting youth retreat so an influential family's son would be eligible. I'm sure he had his reasons, but that was uncomfortable for me. It's hard to live out the truth James gives us, because life constantly pulls on us as we deal with people. But it's a standard that Jesus not only taught, He modeled it. We should do the same.

────────── **So what?** ──────────

1. What distracts you the most—a person's looks, their clothes, their jewelry, their car, or their house?

2. Who have you met that you now admire and value, but weren't struck by their first impression?

3. What kind of person are you tempted to show favor toward?

────────── **Prayer** ──────────

God, it's so hard to see beyond the exterior of a person. Give me the ability to block out those things that distract me so I can see the person you have created, and the gift that he or she is. Amen.

────── **More words from the Word** ──────

1 Samuel 16:7
Matthew 5:3
Romans 2:11
Acts 10:34
Ephesians 6:9
Colossians 3:25

DAY 15

> For the person who keeps all of the laws except one is as guilty as a person who has broken all of God's laws. For the same God who said, "You must not commit adultery," also said, "You must not murder." So if you murder someone but do not commit adultery, you have still broken the law.
>
> *James 2:10–11*

I think we would like it if we had a sin comparison chart. You know, this sin isn't as big as *this* one, and that one isn't as big as *that* one. Then we could feel pretty good about ourselves, because we could always find a way to say, "I'm not *that* big of a sinner." No, wait. We don't need a chart. We say that anyway.

James continues his teaching about favoritism. He wants people to understand this is no small offense that might easily be rationalized away. In fact, James teaches, there are no small offenses. The Jews back then tended to see the law as a ledger kind of deal. If you keep a law, then you get a point on the positive side. If you break a law, you get a point on the negative side. So just keep a positive balance, and you're okay. I bet lots of people think like that today, too.

James straightens that out here. A sin is a sin is a sin. There is no degree of sin, and if you break one, you've broken the law — *all* of it. That makes sense when you think about it. We operate our government that way. All it takes to be a criminal is to get caught breaking one of man's laws. It's the same way in God's Kingdom, too.

God wants total obedience. Partial obedience isn't obedience at all — it's *convenience*. James tells us you don't get to pick which part of God's law you want to follow. God wants you to follow all of it, so you can reap the blessings of the obedient life. But you may respond, "I can't follow all of it, so I won't follow any of it." God says, "I don't want you to miss out on all I have prepared for you. I knew you'd need a way past your imperfection, so I've given you a way of grace. Accept Jesus's death on the cross for your lawlessness. Then obey my laws because they are laws of love." That's tomorrow's lesson.

—————— **So what?** ——————

1.   What sins do you tend to think of as small, less offensive sins?

2.   What sins have you rationalized in your own life?

─────────── **Prayer** ───────────

God, remind me that my sin hurts You and me, and separates me from Your holiness. Help me see that even what I consider a "little" sin cost Jesus his life on the cross for me. Amen.

───── **More words from the Word** ─────

Exodus 20:14
Deuteronomy 27:26
Galatians 3:10

DAY 16

So whatever you say or whatever you do, remember that you will be judged by the law that sets you free. There will be no mercy for those who have not shown mercy to others. But if you have been merciful, God will be merciful when he judges you. *James 2:12–13*

As a kid, I used to laugh at the cartoons when the character would throw a boomerang, and then get clunked in the head when it came back. The cartoon guy was so surprised because he didn't know it was coming. I see a lot of people today who get surprised by a boomerang in the back of the head. They fail to understand the boomerang effect. They may have tossed out the quick fix, the sly deal, the lie, the little sin we talked about yesterday, and BOOM. It comes back to get them later. They get fired for cheating. They lose a business deal or a friend whom they manipulated.

Other people may have been pleasantly surprised by what returned to them, because they tossed out forgiveness, or went out of their way to help someone in need, or sacrificed to give someone they loved a gift. Their boomerang was a blessing from God, in some form or another. Help came when they needed it most. A new friendship came into their life.

Biblically speaking, the boomerang effect is called the law of the harvest—you reap what you sow, and it's evidenced in the way God created the world. You can't get corn if you planted wheat. In the same way, James says, you'll get what you give. If you've not been merciful to others, God will not be merciful to you.

So the opposite is also true: those who are unmerciful will not be shown mercy. Ouch.

If you're a card player, you know what a trump card is. A trump card wins out over whatever it's played against. James reminds us that God's mercy will trump His judgment for those who have been merciful. That's really good news! So go sow mercy.

 So what?

1.   Who needs your mercy? What can you do to extend mercy to them?

2.   What harmful thing are you planting that keeps coming back to hurt you?

3.   What new good thing can you plant in your life?

—————— Prayer ——————

God, forgive me where I have failed to show mercy. Give me the courage to extend it to those who need it from me. Show me where I can plant new seeds of love for Your glory. Amen.

—— More words from the Word ——

Job 22:6
Matthew 6:14–15
Galatians 6:7

DAY 17

> What good is it, dear brothers and sisters, if you say you have faith but don't show it by your actions? Can that kind of faith save anyone? Suppose you see a brother or sister who has no food or clothing, and you say, "Good-bye and have a good day; stay warm and eat well"—but then you don't give that person any food or clothing. What good does that do?
>
> *James 2:14–16*

Knowledge is generally a good thing—except when it comes to faith. Like the scenario James proposes in today's verses, just knowing what you should do doesn't cut it. When it comes to faith, you can't just say, "I'll think about it." Thinking is important, but only if the thinking is the catalyst that turns those thoughts into action. Here's a more frequent cop-out that so many Christians use: "I'll pray for you." Prayer is essential; it is not only the first step, it is the second and third steps. But we then need to go see how God wants us to be the answers to our own prayers.

Martin Luther had a friend who was a Christian as he was, and this friend was also a monk. They came to an agreement. Luther would go down into the dust and heat of the battle for the

Reformation in the world; the friend would stay in the monastery and uphold Luther's hands in prayer. So they began that way. Then, one night, the monk had a dream. He saw a vast field of corn as big as the world, and one solitary man was seeking to reap it—an impossible and a heartbreaking task. Then he caught a glimpse of the reaper's face, and the reaper was Martin Luther. Luther's friend saw the truth in a flash. "I must leave my prayers," he said, "and get to work." And so he left his prayerful solitude and went down to join Luther in his work in the world.

If it can't be observed by an unbelieving world, it's not faith; it's just knowledge. Some people try to make faith a mental exercise or a theological argument. When you have a real, authentic faith, you can't not act. Faith is bound to overflow into action. We'll take another look at faith in action in tomorrow's reading.

———————— So what? ————————

1. What excuses keep you from taking the action step you need to take?

2. Where can you begin to do what you know you should do?

3. Who can you serve that could use your help?

———————————— **Prayer** ——————————

God, catch my tongue when I want to just give lip service to what needs to be done in Your name. Make me like the monk who had to act. Show me what You want me to do, and where I can demonstrate my faith in You and Your ways. Amen.

—————— **More words from the Word** ——————

Matthew 7:21–23
Luke 3:11
1 John 3:17–18

DAY 18

So you see, faith by itself isn't enough.
Unless it produces good deeds, it is dead
and useless.   *James 2:17*

In order to convict someone of a crime there has to be evidence. The same thing is true of substantiating a claim of any sort. You can't file an insurance claim without something to prove you have a right to that claim. To substantiate your claim to be a Jesus follower, James says, there has to be evidence to support that statement. You can't be a "secret Christian." Either the Christianity destroys the secrecy or the secrecy destroys the Christianity.

Check out *The Message*'s paraphrase of this verse: *"Isn't it obvious that God-talk without God-acts is outrageous nonsense?"* Don't just say it; *display* it, James says. There have to be actions that speak, because what we say has no worth unless we have works to back it up. Good works won't substitute for faith, but they do provide evidence of our faith in Christ.[1]

In the 1800s Blondin became well known while still a child as a tightrope artist. As he grew older, his skill and showmanship brought him fame throughout Europe and America. Once in

London he did a somersault on a high wire while wearing stilts. His most spectacular feats were the crossings of Niagara Falls on a tightrope 1,100 feet long and 160 feet above the water. On one occasion he took a stove onto the tightrope and cooked an omelet above the roaring falls. On another occasion he pushed a wheelbarrow across while blindfolded. He obviously entertained the crowds as they watched. He once asked a crowd if they believed he could push someone across safely in the wheelbarrow. The crowd cheered, "Yes! We believe!" So Blondin said, "Who will get in?"

You can say all you want that you believe in Jesus, but if your actions don't prove it, your claims are silenced by the evidence.

─────────── **So what?** ───────────

1.   What area of your life is just God-talk?

2.   How many people who know you well know you're a Christ follower?

─────────── **Prayer** ───────────

God, I pray that my Christian faith will be so authentic that it will give me away as a follower of Jesus. Amen.

—— More words from the Word ——

Galatians 5:6

DAY 19

> Now someone may argue, "Some people
> have faith; others have good deeds." But
> I say, "How can you show me your faith if
> you don't have good deeds? I will show
> you my faith by my good deeds." You say
> you have faith, for you believe that there
> is one God. Good for you! Even the
> demons believe this, and they tremble in
> terror. How foolish! Can't you see that
> faith without good deeds is useless?
>
> *James 2:18–20*

When I was a youth pastor, one of my favorite youth ministry outings was the Spy Game. The Spy Game entails going to a busy public place, like a mall, and each person picks a different someone to spy on. You then follow your subject at a safe distance so they won't notice you stalking them (I would always tell the kids, if mall security stops to ask what you're doing, I don't know you). Then you make mental notes to see how much you can learn about them, just by observing their actions. If they shop in certain stores, then you can begin to deduce things about them, based on the amount of money they spend, and what they spend it on. You could tell what they like to eat when they go to the food court. You can gather more information if you see what kind of car they get into as they nervously leave to escape you.

It's just the truth: the only measure of what you believe is what you do. Actions speak louder than words. If you want to know who I am, watch what I do. If I want to know who you are, all I have to do is watch what you do. The funny thing about us as humans is we tend to say one thing and do another. It gets worse. We even have a familiar phrase—I think a parent made it up: "Do as I say and not as I do."

We have heard God's message, and we say we believe. Most people have gotten that far. Most people believe that a God exists who created the universe. Most believe that God loves them. Most celebrate Christmas as the birthday of Jesus the Christ. That's head knowledge. But WHAM! James says even the demons have head knowledge like that.

For authentic, vital faith, we must make the 18-inch journey from head knowledge to heart knowledge. Heart knowledge cannot just say belief is enough. We *must* find a way to demonstrate what we believe, because we are compelled to act out. James says, "Now that's what I'm talking about!"

——————— **So what?** ———————

1. What can people learn about you by watching you today?

2. What beliefs do you hold that need to be reexamined?

——————— **Prayer** ———————

God, I want to be a shining light for You. Help me see where I can be more congruent in my words and actions. Thank You for loving me, even when I'm inconsistent. Amen.

—— **More words from the Word** ——

Matthew 5:14–16
Colossians 1:6
Hebrews 6:10

DAY 20

Don't you remember that our ancestor Abraham was shown to be right with God by his actions when he offered his son Isaac on the altar? You see, his faith and his actions worked together. His actions made his faith complete. And so it happened just as the Scriptures say: "Abraham believed God, and God counted him as righteous because of his faith." He was even called the friend of God. So you see, we are shown to be right with God by what we do, not by faith alone. Rahab the prostitute is another example. She was shown to be right with God by her actions when she hid those messengers and sent them safely away by a different road.   *James 2:21–25*

You've got to hear Abraham's story. He was old. His wife was old, and they had no children. Yet God had promised him that he would be a father of many descendants, as many as the stars in the heavens. And Abraham believed God. Sure enough, Sarah became pregnant and gave birth to Isaac when Abraham was 101 and Sarah was 80.

When Isaac was a young boy, God told Abraham to go to a mountaintop and sacrifice Isaac, who was still his only son. You can figure this one out. No son, no descendants. But nevertheless, the next morning, Abraham got an early start. He told Isaac that God would provide a lamb for the sacrifice. Abraham even got to the point of raising the knife above his only son on the rock altar. God saw Abraham's faithfulness, and called out for him to stop. Abraham was willing to obey, even when it defied logic.

James says that Abraham was "declared right" for what he *did*. He believed, and he obeyed because he believed.

Sometimes, God calls us to act in faith that defies our logical mind. Many times ministry is that kind of white-knuckled faith ride. I can only imagine what Abraham was thinking as he hiked with Isaac to the mountaintop that day. He could find no logic in God's plan, but he did what God told him to do. Many times in our faith journeys, we will experience that same kind of "Okay, God" moment. It may mean moving to another city. Perhaps it may mean staying for a while longer in a marriage you feel is over. All because we sense that's what God is telling us to do. God always shows up, and we then wonder why we were concerned.

It's not faith until we have to use it; until then, it's only knowledge.

———————— So what? ————————

1. What can you learn from Abraham's faith?

2. How have you seen God show up when you've been faithful?

3. In what area of your life do you need to allow God to lead you that you've been unwilling to go before?

———————— Prayer ————————

God, hold me in Your grip when I tremble because I can't see what You're up to. Give me more faith to do what You command, especially when it defies every bit of logic from my point of view. Amen.

—— More words from the Word ——

Genesis 22:1–14
Joshua 2; 6:20–25

DAY 21

Here's the conclusion, just in case you didn't get it, James says. He told us what he was going to say, he said it, and now he's telling us what he said. If there's no spirit in the body, there's no life anymore. If there are no good deeds to prove the faith, there's no faith. True faith, James says, will grow and develop and breathe life into the body so others can see the life within.

Here's a helpful chart to see what results a living faith brings:[1]

Faith described as:	Results in:
Tested (1:2,3)	Patience (1:3)
Without doubt (1:6-8)	Answered prayer (1:5)
Enduring temptation (1:12)	Eternal life (1:12)
More than belief (2:19,20)	Faith perfected by works (2:22)
Believing God (2:23-25)	Righteousness before God (2:23)

James said it long before Nike did: Just do it.

―――――――― **So what?** ――――――――

1. What fruit are you growing?

2. What fruit are you lacking?

―――――――― **Prayer** ――――――――

God, create in me a desire to grow more faith, that I can produce more fruit, and to serve You because of all You have done for me. Let these scriptural truths encourage me to let my light shine boldly, knowing You will provide where You guide. Amen.

―――― **More words from the Word** ――――

James 2:14
James 2:17
James 2:20

DAY 22

> Dear brothers and sisters, not many of you should become teachers in the church, for we who teach will be judged more strictly.
>
> *James 3:1*

Among the various part-time jobs I've had in my life, perhaps the most interesting one was working in a Christian cable TV studio while I was in grad school. Now don't think the set of CNN or ESPN—quite the opposite. This "studio" was about 10 feet by 20 feet, and that included the tech "booth" and the set, and the door to the office building hallway opened into this one room. My job was to come in on weeknights, broadcast the local programming, and switch back to the national satellite feed after a few hours. I just had to monitor the sound and picture for quality, so I mainly did my own schoolwork and paid minimal attention to the local preachers who were teaching. I generally closed my books with a few minutes left in the last local show.

And, bless his heart (here in the South, you can say anything you want about someone if you preface your comments with this phrase), this one guy was terrible. His theology was incorrect, and his preparation was nil. In fact, all of the local guys were pitiful—bless their hearts. They each taped four half-hour shows for the week, back to back in one morning, and then do it again the next week. They shot from the hip as the camera rolled, and they'd throw in a few "Well, hallelujah, thank you Jesus"es while they thought of something else to talk about.

That's the kind of teacher James is speaking about in today's verse. Remember this Christian church thing is brand new and busting at the seams, with house churches springing up everywhere. There were lots of people teaching who were untrained, unlike the professional rabbis they had all grown accustomed to in the Jewish synagogues. Often the floor was open for others to speak. In fact, the apostle Paul used this privilege to speak as a guest in different cities. James is speaking to those who just liked to listen to themselves speak or take the opportunity to filibuster for a while.

Teaching the faith is a great responsibility, to be careful to instruct the accurate basics of this new faith. James is saying that teaching could be a dangerous role, so be sure and handle it appropriately.

That word is for all of us in some way, because as we grow spiritually, people will submit to us, even subtly, for direction in the faith. We need to be sure we understand the importance of communicating the truth in our words, and in our lives. People are watching, whether we think they are or not.

─────────── **So what?** ───────────

1.   Who has taught you well in the faith? Consider letting them know how grateful you are!

2.   Who looks to you for guidance, that you can influence with your witness?

─────────── **Prayer** ───────────

God, I pray that I'll represent you well to those who are watching and listening to me. Remind me what a privilege it is to tell others about You and what You've done for me. Amen.

─── **More words from the Word:** ───

Matthew 23:8
Romans 2:21
1 Timothy 1:7

Indeed, we all make ma...
we could control our to...
be perfect and could al...
selves in every other wa...
large horse go wherever w...
means of a small bit in its mouth. And a
small rudder makes a huge ship turn
wherever the pilot chooses to go, even
though the winds are strong. In the same
way, the tongue is a small thing that
makes grand speeches. But a tiny spark
can set a great forest on fire. *James 3:2–5*

One of my favorite comics is *Calvin and Hobbes*. Calvin is a precocious early elementary aged kid, and Hobbes is his stuffed-animal tiger, who comes to life only in the solitary presence of Calvin. In one strip, Calvin is at school during recess, and tells the class bully, "You better be nice to me, Moe, because someday my tax dollars will be paying for your prison cell." In the next frame, Moe punches Calvin's lights out. The last frame has Calvin lying in a heap, mumbling, "My whole problem is my lips move when I think." That's the challenge for most of us, too. We too often speak first, then think, and it causes us and others a world of trouble.

our words are coming out sometimes, we be thinking, "Uh-oh."

James says he faces the same challenge, too. He says we all make many mistakes with our tongues. In the same way Jesus did, James uses some simple, well-understood objects to make his point. A bit on an animal bridle, a rudder on a ship, and the human tongue — all are small, but they can give direction to a much larger entity. If we can control our tongue, James teaches, we can control ourselves in every way.

The tongue has terrifying potential to do a lot of damage, James says. Before you and I speak, we must remember that harmful words are like fire — we can neither control nor reverse the damage they do.[1] James isn't telling us to keep our mouths shut. What he is telling us is the importance of keeping our tongue under control, to prevent it from being like the spark that starts a devastating forest fire.

—————— So what? ——————

1. When have you been the victim of someone's damaging tongue? Does the effect of that damage still linger in some way?

2. When or with whom are you most likely to say some out-of-control, hurtful things?

3.   What steps can you take to control your tongue a little better today?

 Prayer

Oh God, thank you for the power of the tongue to communicate. I pray I will use this incredible responsibility wisely, for good and not for damaging evil. Just for today, Lord, I pray for improvement. Amen.

More words from the Word

Psalm 34:13
Proverbs 5:2
Proverbs 10:19
Matthew 12:34–37

DAY 24

And the tongue is a flame of fire. It is a whole world of wickedness, corrupting your entire body. It can set your whole life on fire, for it is set on fire by hell itself. People can tame all kinds of animals, birds, reptiles, and fish, but no one can tame the tongue. It is restless and evil, full of deadly poison. *James 3:6–8*

People like me who grew up way back when remember the often-shown TV commercials featuring Smokey the Bear. (Smokey is now 70 years old!) Smokey would teach all of us little kids about not playing with matches, and his big line was, "Only *you* can prevent forest fires."

James could have used that line himself, because that's his underlying message in today's verses. James says our tongues can become strategic weapons for Satan, to do his divisive work. And we can launch missiles from far away; we don't even have to be in mouth-to-mouth combat. When we don't watch what we say, the untamed tongue goes wild in spewing poisonous talk. We gossip, put others down, brag, manipulate, spread false teaching, exaggerate, complain, patronize, lie, and slander. And that's just what *we* start.

What happens when we bring our untamed tongue to a less than honorable discussion? Do we make a bad situation worse? We have to realize our words in a volatile situation are either like a bucket of gasoline, or bucket of water. They either add fuel to the fire, or they help extinguish the blaze.

James says no one can control the tongue. We as humans constantly demonstrate we can't handle our tongues under our own power. It might be easy to just give up, and not even try. But it's important to work at it, because it's better to fight fires than to go around and set new ones. And God's power is there to help us control the tongue and use it for good.

———————— So what? ————————

1. What kind of bucket do you usually bring to a volatile conversation?

2. How often do you ask for God's help in controlling your tongue?

3. Where can you intentionally use your words to build up someone today?

———————— Prayer ————————

God, I need Your help with my tongue. Step in and get my attention when I'm in an influential situation, so I can build people up, and not tear them down. Amen.

—— More words from the Word ——

Psalm 120:2,3
Psalm 140:3
Proverbs 16:27
Ecclesiastes 10:11
Romans 3:13

DAY 25

Sometimes it praises our Lord and Father, and sometimes it curses those who have been made in the image of God. And so blessing and cursing come pouring out of the same mouth. Surely, my brothers and sisters, this is not right! Does a spring of water bubble out with both fresh water and bitter water? Does a fig tree produce olives, or a grapevine produce figs? No, and you can't draw fresh water from a salty spring. James 3:9–12

President Ulysses Grant wined and dined Chief Red Cloud and other Native Indian chiefs of the Sioux tribes as he showed them a map of how the Dakota regions would be "rearranged" to benefit them. Red Cloud and the other chiefs understood very little of the proposal of the white men from Washington, but he was able to communicate his opinion of the whole deal through sign language. He stuck out his fist with his index and middle fingers in a *V* formation. This wasn't the Indian sign for "victory"; it was the sign for "forked tongue," or "lies."

James accuses those in the church of having forked tongues, too. What can you believe to be the truth, when conflicting words come from the same person? John Bunyan, in *The Pilgrim's Progress,* tells us of Talkative: "He was a saint abroad and a devil at home."[1] How many times have we seen someone be like this, speaking so kindly to complete strangers, and yet use sharp, hurtful language when speaking to those in his own family! Who is he then, really? It's hard to tell. You could make a case based on the evidence for both a loving person and a horrible father.

Remember the old horror story, *Dr. Jekyll and Mr. Hyde?* Dr. Jekyll drinks this mysterious potion, and is transformed into the diabolical Mr. Hyde. Sometimes, we as Jesus followers look like that. We make excuses for our behavior and speech, saying it wasn't "really" us. We have to take responsibility for who we are and what we say, James says, *all* the time, not just when it's convenient. He says it just cannot be. Stop being a snake and use your tongue only for good.

———————— So what? ————————

1. Are you a "different person" depending upon who you're with?

2. What percentage of your words reflect poorly on the kind of person you want to be?

———————— **Prayer** ————————

God, let my words be consistently pleas-ing to You today, like a spring of fresh, clean water. Amen.

—— **More words from the Word** ——

Genesis 1:26
Genesis 5:1
Genesis 9:6
1 Corinthians 11:7

DAY 26

> If you are wise and understand God's ways, prove it by living an honorable life, doing good works with the humility that comes from wisdom. But if you are bitterly jealous and there is selfish ambition in your heart, don't cover up the truth with boasting and lying. For jealousy and selfishness are not God's kind of wisdom. Such things are earthly, unspiritual, and demonic. For wherever there is jealousy and selfish ambition, there you will find disorder and evil of every kind. *James 3:13–16*

Some time ago, I ran across a very funny web site, called *Bozo Criminal of the Day*. Each day, a stupid criminal report is posted. It's full of dumb people doing something they actually thought was a smart idea. Here's a sample: [1]

> Bozo criminals for today are from Indian Shores, Florida. They had some pot and they needed to sell it so they hatched a plan. 1. Obtain a van. 2. Load with an ample supply of pot. 3. Include the tools of the trade, including a digital scale, rolling papers and zip top plastic bags. 4. Find a nice open area to park and set up shop. After doing all this, item number five was added to the list. 5. Take a nap. But it wasn't the nap that really sealed

their fate. It was the nice open area they decided to park in. It was the police department parking lot. Oops. They're busted.

These bozos, of course, think they are wise, but their actions say otherwise. James is writing these verses to some similar bozos. He warns those who want to trumpet to the world that they have wisdom, but instead harbor contradictory attitudes and actions, like jealousy and envy. He is especially concerned about those who teach, as he stated in the beginning of the chapter (Day 22). James commands that they live lives of steady goodness that will produce only good deeds. If there's no goodness on the inside, you won't be able to produce it on the outside. Don't think you can disguise your thoughts to pass them off as godly wisdom, James says. What's on the inside of a person will come forth to show his true colors. And if it's bitterness and envy, then it's clearly not from God's kind of wisdom. Far from it — it's of the Devil, and it will always manifest itself in disorder and other kinds of evil. And disorder will do the exact opposite of what God wants and provides through His wisdom.

——————— So what? ———————

1.   What bad habits or attitudes do you hold on to that work against the wisdom you want and need in your life?

Greg Griffin   75

2.   Is there an area of disorder in your life that is an indicator of something that's out of alignment in your spirit?

Prayer

God, help me to see where I'm apt to brag, or to be more concerned about my selfish needs. Replace those areas in my life with habits that will lead to true wisdom. Amen.

More words from the Word

Galatians 6:4
Romans 13:13
Philippians 3:19
1 Corinthians 3:3

DAY 27

But the wisdom from above is first of all pure. It is also peace loving, gentle at all times, and willing to yield to others. It is full of mercy and good deeds. It shows no favoritism and is always sincere. *James 3:17*

Wow! This is a rich verse about true wisdom, and it's in sharp contrast to the supposed "wisdom" of those James targeted in the last few verses. We don't have to be confused about what is wisdom and what is not. Real wisdom will bear itself out in good deeds and righteous living. Here's a great checklist for our next big challenge when we need a heavy dose of wisdom.

"Wisdom from God" checklist from James 3:17

___ is empty of ulterior and selfish motives

___ creates right relationships

___ exercises uncommon reason

___ has a knack for knowing when to yield

___ shows compassion that moves quickly to action

___ remains clear about the truth

___ is transparent and authentic

Remember back in Day 3's Scripture? James says this kind of wisdom is available for you and me if we just ask God for it. That's a cool God who shares that kind of valuable commodity with His children!

I like this quote from a respected writer and pastor, J.I. Packer: "Wisdom is the power to see and the inclination to choose the best and highest goal, together with the surest means of attaining it."[1] That sounds like Godly wisdom to me. And it also sounds very appealing.

So what?

1. What decisions are you facing right now that need Godly wisdom?

2. Which description from the checklist seems the most helpful to you for those decisions?

Prayer

God, Your wisdom is so irresistible when I see it in light of this Scripture. I pray for a hunger to receive as much as I can hold. Continue to pour out Your wisdom on my life, and I pray I'll be able to share it with others, for Your glory. Amen.

—— **More words from the Word** ——

Romans 12:9
1 Corinthians 2:6,7

DAY 28

You have probably heard of Johnny Appleseed. He was a real person named John Chapman who was born in 1776. As a young man in his twenties, he was among the very first Americans to explore the rich, new territory west of the Ohio River. He got his name because of his apple tree planting mission. Chapman, who was a dedicated Christian, caught a vision of the new wilderness blossoming with orchards of apple trees that would produce a continual harvest for new settlers, and he willingly endured a hard backcountry life as he worked to make his dream come true. There is no way to estimate how many millions of seeds he planted in the hundreds of nurseries he created in the territory lying south of the Great Lakes and between the Ohio and Mississippi Rivers. Many of those trees continue to bear apples even today.

Johnny Appleseed was a dedicated planter, and James calls his readers to be dedicated planters as well. James says we need to be planting seeds of peace that will produce a harvest of goodness.

James says not everyone will be a peacemaker, but the reward is great for those who are. When it all comes down, in every situation, you only have two options: be a peacemaker . . . or not. If you do decide to be a peacemaker, then the job is simple: sow seeds of peace. Who can know the harvest your one seed of peace will produce? It might re-produce a hundredfold, because in God's economy, a little can become a lot.

So what?

1.   What field has God given to you for planting seeds of peace?

2.   Imagine what could happen if you become a peace planter on a regular basis.

Prayer

God, may I be inspired by Your servant John Chapman's single-minded vision, so I'll become known as a planter of Your peace. Amen.

More words from the Word

Proverbs 11:18
Isaiah 32:17
Hosea 10:12
Amos 6:12

DAY 29

> What is causing the quarrels and fights among you? Don't they come from the evil desires at war within you? You want what you don't have, so you scheme and kill to get it. You are jealous of what others have, but you can't get it, so you fight and wage war to take it away from them. Yet you don't have what you want because you don't ask God for it. And even when you ask, you don't get it because your motives are all wrong—you want only what will give you pleasure.
>
> *James 4:1-3*

Go ahead. Admit it. You've seen at least a part of one *Jerry Springer* show. If you've ever stumbled upon it while surfing channels, you find yourself watching at least for a brief moment, for no other reason than out of sheer disbelief. You wonder, "Where do they get these people?" These aren't actors; these are real people with some real messed-up lives. People actually want to get on TV to scream and fight with each other. Sadly, that's who they are. They really live like that.

James must have known some *Jerry Springer*–type people. He addresses some greedy schemers, jealous coveters—who are in the church! As we have seen by now, James's style is very direct. He says, let's get right to the root of the trouble: it's all your wrong, evil desires. And evil desires are always a threat to your spirit life with God. Wrong desires will always damage your relationships and drive you to shameful deeds. James teaches, stop looking for love in all the wrong places. What you really want and need, you can only get from God.

And James doesn't let up. You have not because you ask not, James says. You need to ask God. But, you can't ask Him like you ask Santa Claus—gimme, gimme, gimme. God won't give you whatever you want just so you can fulfill your pleasures. He loves you too much to do that. We have to ask with a pure motive, and when we do, God will give us what we need. And proper praying always brings proper perspective. The more we pray, the more we learn how to pray according to God's desires, not our own.

———————— So what? ————————

1. What can your recent conflicts tell you about the purity of your desires?

2. What have you prayed for lately that may have been out of selfish desires?

—————————— **Prayer** ——————————

God, purify my heart today so my pray-
ers will be pleasing to You, and a blessing to
me and those I pray for. Amen.

—— **More words from the Word** ——

Matthew 6:9,10
Romans 7:23
Galatians 5:17
1 John 2:15

DAY 30

You adulterers! Don't you realize that friendship with the world makes you an enemy of God? I say it again: If you want to be a friend of the world, you make yourself an enemy of God. What do you think the Scriptures mean when they say that the spirit God has placed within us is filled with envy?   James 4:4–5

How do you respond when someone calls you a name? It gets your attention, for sure. It's just a guess, but I'm thinking James got some attention when he called those who are into their own desires "adulterers." That's a pretty strong word, huh? He's using a well-understood, vivid image to describe spiritual adultery. All through the Old Testament, it's clear that any idol worship was spiritual adultery against God, taking people away from the right covenant relationship. Turning one's heart to something other than God is like breaking the marriage vow. Our relationship with God isn't a functional one, like a boss and employee; it's a close, intimate one, like a marriage. When we sin, we break God's heart, just like one marriage partner's heart gets broken by the desertion of the other.[1]

James says you have to choose—God or the world. I bet he was recalling the words of his brother Jesus, "No man can serve two masters" (Matthew 6:24). You can't have two lovers without cheating on them both. If you want to chase the desires of this world, you aren't God's friend, because your heart's not after the same things. That's why James says God is jealous, because His love is just that strong for you and me, and God knows that no other god can satisfy us. Out of that deep love for us, God doesn't want to see us joined with anyone but Him. How special does that make you feel, that the God of the Universe is so passionate to love you that He would be jealous if you rejected His love?

God wants us to enjoy the world that He has made and given for our enjoyment. He just doesn't want us to pervert the gift by worshiping it more than the Giver.

—————— **So what?** ——————

1. What areas of your life do you have trouble putting in proper priority?

2. What steps can you take to keep from injuring your relationship with God?

—————— Prayer ——————

God, thank you that You love me with a jealous love that does not let me go. I pray that, with Your help, I'll make sure I don't let any evil desire in me keep me from You and Your love. Amen.

—— More words from the Word ——

Romans 8:7
Galatians 1:4
Genesis 6:5

DAY 31

But he gives us even more grace to stand against such evil desires. As the Scriptures say, "God opposes the proud but favors the humble." So humble yourselves before God. Resist the devil, and he will flee from you.   *James 4:6–7*

Yesterday's reading drove home the truth that God is a very jealous God, and He doesn't want us to be unfaithful to Him. You might be thinking, "If God is like that, how can I give Him the devotion he demands?" Don't worry, James says. God gives you what you need. If the lure of the world is pulling harder on you, God will give you even more strength to equal what you'll need.

The trouble with being human is we often too easily take the Devil's bait. He whispers, "You can do it all by yourself. You don't need any help from anyone else." We begin to believe it. We begin to think, "I'm pretty sharp. Hey, I'm a player. I really *don't* need anybody." And BAM! We fall down and we can't get up, because we're not strong enough in our own power to deal with everything that comes and finds us. That's why James quotes Proverbs 3:34. If you try to be God, then you end up finding out fairly quickly that you are not Him—

the hard way. If you're not humble, you'll stumble. The Greek word for "proud" is *huperephanos,* which literally means "one who shows himself above other people."[1] Pride says, "It's all about me." Humility says, "Woe is me—I know I need God."

If you're having a problem connecting with God, it's probably a pride thing. Here's a good indication of where you're proud—you are overly sensitive to criticism in that area. Where you see no need, you see no need for Jesus. But when we admit the truth that we are not strong enough to stand against even our own evil desires, we are then willing to seek help. God says, "That's where I come in, if you'll allow Me." Our humility opens the door to receive God's power and strength to resist the Devil. It's there for the taking, if we'll let go of any pride we might have, and receive it.

--- **So what?** ---

1.   In what area of your life do you feel like you're self-sufficient?

2.   What lessons have you learned the hard way from being too prideful?

3.   Whom do you admire because of their humility?

─────────── **Prayer** ───────────

O God, do whatever it takes to break my pride, so it won't separate me from You or from the things You want me to do. Amen.

──── **More words from the Word** ────

Matthew 5:3
Matthew 23:12
Ephesians 4:27
1 Peter 5:8

DAY 32

Come close to God, and God will come close to you. Wash your hands, you sinners; purify your hearts, for your loyalty is divided between God and the world. Let there be tears for what you have done. Let there be sorrow and deep grief. Let there be sadness instead of laughter, and gloom instead of joy. Humble yourselves before the Lord, and he will lift you up in honor.   *James 4:8–10*

It's an amazing thing that hundreds of airplanes travel daily, coast-to-coast, overseas, at night, or even in a thick fog, and still get to their chosen destinations! As important as a flight plan is, that's not the key to keeping the plane on its course. In fact, during a flight the plane is *off* course more than it is *on* course. Air turbulence, rain, air traffic, and human error all knock the plane off course from time to time. The key is staying in tune with the plane's instrument gauges and the control towers, both of which are rooted in the unchanging, absolute GPS parameters of the environment. Those parameters provide the necessary information to allow the pilots to make the corrections to get back on course. Just like an airplane in flight, we need to stay close to God and his teachings if we are to stay "on course" in our Christian walk.

You've probably seen the bumper sticker: *If you feel like God is far away, guess who moved?* James says, when *you* move closer again, you'll find that God is already very close. He was right there all along, waiting for your attention. God has already made the first move by letting us know how much He loves us by sending Jesus to die on the cross for your sin and mine. Because he loves us that much, He respects our ability and privilege to respond without pressure. So He watches and waits, just like the father of the lost son in Jesus's story (John 15). And when you come to Him, He runs out to greet you and welcome you once again.

When you draw close, James says, clean your hands and your heart so you can see God clearly again. Get rid of any filth that may have gotten into your life. You might need to shed a few tears of sorrow for your wrong actions or wrong words, because you can't enjoy the truth of your forgiveness in God's grace until you've acknowledged the heartache of your sin that you need to release.

Then, James says, good news! When you draw close to God with a sincere heart and receive again His grace and love, you may encounter a paradox—you might expect that you'll have to grovel to get your way back into God's good graces. God says just the opposite: "No, my child. I will *honor* you, for your humble spirit is to be celebrated." Do you get James's point, that humility is the key?

―――――――― **So what?** ――――――――

1.   At a time when you felt far away from God, what caused you to realize it?

2.   Why is humility harder to practice than pride?

―――――――― **Prayer** ――――――――

God, show me that any remorse I will feel in order to move closer to You is greater than the pain I'll experience if I continue to stay away. Thank you for Your standing, open invitation to draw close to You any time I need to. Amen.

―― **More words from the Word** ――

Job 22:29
Proverbs 29:3
Isaiah 57:15
Luke 15:20-24
1 Peter 5:6

DAY 33

> Don't speak evil against each other, dear brothers and sisters. If you criticize and judge each other, then you are criticizing and judging God's law. But your job is to obey the law, not to judge whether it applies to you. God alone, who gave the law, is the Judge. He alone has the power to save or to destroy. So what right do you have to judge your neighbor? *James 4:11–12*

There have always been a bunch of TV shows about courts of law, all the way back to *Perry Mason* in the days of black-and-white TV. We seem fascinated by judges, juries, and the whole process. So much so that the networks keep giving us more court shows. We can now be entertained as we watch real-life disputes get resolved in courtrooms on shows like *The People's Court*. Sometimes, the defendant will directly challenge the judge, and it doesn't take a top-notch attorney to know that's a *big* mistake. The first rule of court is: *you* are not the judge—don't forget it.

James is getting that very same truth across in today's verses. He says that when you don't treat your brothers and sisters with love, and instead you condemn and criticize them, you are taking the law into your own hands. Why? Because you are violating God's supreme law for relation-ships—love Me and love your neighbor. Period. You're challenging the Judge by doing it your way instead of God's way. God says you're disobeying Me because you won't follow what I have estab-lished. It's not up for discussion. I want you to obey Me. And you're violating My law in a second way by acting as if it's your right to condemn and pass judgment on your neighbor. Like *you're* per-fect, James says. No one has that right but God. James asks another of his penetrating rhetorical questions: so who are you to judge? When we judge, we condemn ourselves. James teaches us, don't forget the first rule of our God: you are not the Judge.

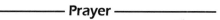

So what?

1.   Whom or in what situation do you have a hard time not judging?

2.   When is a time you remember feel-ing the repercussions of judgment, from someone else to you, and from you to someone else?

Prayer

God, replace my thoughts of judgment toward someone else today with thoughts of encouragement and care for them. Help me remember it's not my job to make a statement on everything and about everybody. Amen.

—— More words from the Word ——

Matthew 7:1–5
2 Corinthians 12:20
Ephesians 4:31
1 Peter 2:1–3

DAY 34

> Look here, you who say, "Today or tomorrow we are going to a certain town and will stay there a year. We will do business there and make a profit." How do you know what your life will be like tomorrow? Your life is like the morning fog—it's here a little while, then it's gone. What you ought to say is, "If the Lord wants us to, we will live and do this or that." Otherwise you are boasting about your own plans, and all such boasting is evil.
>
> *James 4:13–16*

James has a lot to work on with this crowd—first arguing, then judging, and now bragging. He's on a roll now, so he fires off another pointed question: what makes you think you know about tomorrow? He tells a quick parable in much the same way Jesus did in Luke 12 to make this simple truth clear: Our time is not our time.

Our time is a gift, not a given. In God's grand design of things, the time we have here on this planet is but a small vapor mist in the span of the indescribable cosmos, James says. How long do we have here? Only God knows. He has His good reasons, even though we may never understand them.

We have to remember that time is only for this planet. Beyond here, time is non-existent. Eternity isn't a time dimension. It's a timeless dimension. You can read about Albert Einstein's theory of relativity that supports this truth—if you can hang with him. Eternity is one big, fat now—no yesterday, no tomorrow. (It's perfect for procrastinators!) Everything happens in the unending present moment.

James says, so stop boasting. There you go playing God again. As I like to say, you want to make God laugh? Tell Him your plans. What you *should* say is this: if the Lord is willing, *then* we will live and do this or that. I love the balance there. God doesn't say, "Don't make any plans because whatever is going to happen will happen." He says, "Make plans, and then you'll be prepared, but then place those plans in My Almighty hands before you even think about them any longer." That's where they really are anyway.

Yesterday is history. Tomorrow is a mystery. Today is a gift—that's why we call it the present.

———————— So what? ————————

1.   What are you most likely to boast about?

2.   How can you make sure you include God's plans in your plans today?

3.   What can you best do with your time today?

 **Prayer**

Thank You, Lord, for each moment You give me here on this planet. Forgive me when I run ahead of You. Remind me You have a far better place waiting for Me if I will give my life and my time here to You. Amen.

More words from the Word

Psalm 102:3
Proverbs 27:1
Luke 12:16–21

DAY 35

It's easy and sleazy to just turn your head when you know you should do the right thing. It might be a simple task, but you're too lazy. It might be an uncomfortable task, but you're too afraid. It's been said there are two sins: sins of commission and sins of omission. Check this out: Misdeeds are sins of commission, and missed deeds are sins of omission.

Several years ago, the Christian rock group DC Talk wrote a song called "Jesus Freak," about standing up for the ways of Jesus regardless of what people would think. It birthed a partnership with Voice of the Martyrs,[1] a group that tells the story of Christians around the world who simply did what they knew they should, even when it was unpopular or dangerous. Their stories are compiled in a book titled *Jesus Freaks*. In the book's introduction, Michael Tait (then of DC Talk) explains the book's purpose: "In a world built on free will instead of God's will, we must be the Freaks. While we may not be called to martyr our lives, we must martyr our way of life. We must put our self-ish ways to death and march to a different beat. Then the world will see Jesus."[2]

Sometimes doing the right thing could cost us, but perhaps not as much as not doing the right thing.

James says, okay, now you know, so don't plead innocence. Just do it.

────────── **So what?** ──────────

1.   When have you recently passed over an opportunity to do the right thing?

2.   What are your usual excuses that you might use to rationalize inaction?

3.   What steps can you take to be ready for your next "God opportunity"?

────────── **Prayer** ──────────

Lord, forgive my lame excuses and misplaced priorities. Prod me the next time I'm tempted to let the opportunity pass without acting on Your behalf. Thank you for loving me regardless. Amen.

────── **More words from the Word** ──────

Luke 12:47
John 9:41
2 Peter 2:21

DAY 36

> Look here, you rich people: Weep and groan with anguish because of all the terrible troubles ahead of you. Your wealth is rotting away, and your fine clothes are moth-eaten rags. Your gold and silver have become worthless. The very wealth you were counting on will eat away your flesh like fire. This treasure you have accumulated will stand as evidence against you on the day of judgment. For listen! Hear the cries of the field workers whom you have cheated of their pay. The wages you held back cry out against you. The cries of those who harvest your fields have reached the ears of the Lord of Heaven's Armies. You have spent your years on earth in luxury, satisfying your every desire. You have fattened yourselves for the day of slaughter. You have condemned and killed innocent people, who do not resist you.
>
> *James 5:1–6*

Enron. WorldCom. Lehman Brothers. Bernie Madoff. These are just some of the more recently exposed greed machines. And it's just a matter of time before those who haven't been found out yet are exposed, too. Greed isn't a new problem, or just an American problem. It's been around for a long time, and it's one of the Devil's most effective tools to ruin people. So you'd figure James would have a word on the subject. Oh yeah he does.

James calls out to the rich, "Hey! You! Yeah, I'm talking to *you*." And then from there he really piles it on. If you only knew, he writes, you'd be *shrieking* in anguish for what's ahead. You're just like a fat lazy animal that doesn't know he's the main entrée for the party tomorrow night. He says this isn't a rags-to-riches tale; it's a riches-to-rags tale.

Wealth isn't the problem for James; greed is. There's a big difference. He's sending a message to those who will do anything to make a buck so they can live the life of luxury. In that day, most laborers lived hand to mouth, day by day. If a shady boss cheated them out of a few days' pay, they literally would be on the edge of starvation. James says you evil people are going to get what's coming to you. Just as a reminder, this was a letter to the people in the church.

James's goal is to keep those who read his letter from putting their hopes on earthly things. He wants them to know where real treasure is — in God. Sir Fred Catherwood said, "Greed is the logical result of the belief that there is no life after death. We grab what we can while we can however we can and then hold on to it hard."[1]

Greed can happen to anyone, so don't let the love of money ruin you. Yeah, I'm talking to *you*.

———————— **So what?** ————————

1.   On the greedy (1) to generous (10) scale, where would you rank yourself?

2.   Where do you tend to overindulge?

———————— **Prayer** ————————

God, keep me from the love of money. Show me how I can manage what You give me wisely and leverage it for the things of Heaven. Amen.

——— **More words from the Word** ———

Proverbs 11:28
Matthew 6:19
1 Timothy 6:9,10

DAY 37

Dear brothers and sisters, be patient as you wait for the Lord's return. Consider the farmers who patiently wait for the rains in the fall and in the spring. They eagerly look for the valuable harvest to ripen. You, too, must be patient. Take courage, for the coming of the Lord is near. Don't grumble about each other, brothers and sisters, or you will be judged. For look—the Judge is standing at the door!   *James 5:7–9*

Atlanta traffic. Enough said, huh? If you don't live in Atlanta, you don't want to know. Even getting back and forth in residential areas can be brutal. I've not always been the most patient person in the world when I get behind the wheel of my car. Impatience and driving are not a real good combination. I try to find every little side road, every little trick I can to shave precious minutes off of my drive times.

One of my favorite discoveries of all time was that I could bypass a very long line of cars by driving in the middle turn lane with my blinker on, pretending I was about to turn. Pretty good, huh? But as luck would have it, I sensed a bigger twinge of guilt after every successful evasion. I felt God was saying, "Are you that important that you need to break the law to get ahead of everybody else?" "Okay, God." He won, and I don't do that anymore . . . except in extenuating circumstances. I'm working on it, okay?!

James says be patient; just be patient. What a change of attitude! James's anger at the greedy quickly turns to consolation and encouragement for fellow believers. He says the greedy think about the short run and just live for today, but you should think about the long run, and be patient. Look at the farmer for encouragement, James says. Just like the farmer has to first prepare the soil, then plant the seed, then water the seed, and *then* let the seed grow to its full measure — only then the farmer can enjoy the fruit of the harvest. James says the farmer knows there's no shortcut even if he wanted a shortcut. So just . . . be patient.

Sometimes it's easier to be patient if you can see why you need to be patient. Here's why. Jesus is coming again when it's the right time. And in the meantime, let that perspective guide you and what you do.

So don't live as if He's not coming back. James says, Don't spend your energy and time on the petty stuff I've had to correct you about in my writings. When Jesus comes, we need to be in rich fellowship, excited to see Him, not in quarrels and confusion, looking sheepish. I love what a friend of mine used to say. He says if the church universal keeps going the way it's going, Jesus could come back, and sigh, "Is this the best you people could do?"

Get on with the things of the Kingdom. Lay aside everything else; it's just fluff.

So what?

1.   What earthly thing is your biggest stumbling block to keeping a patient, heavenly perspective?

2.   What do you need to let go of that just doesn't matter?

Prayer

God, give me discernment for what's petty and what's not. Help me to keep the petty things in perspective, and be willing to let them go for the sake of what You want me to do with my time and thoughts. Amen.

More words from the Word

Jeremiah 5:24
Romans 13:11,12
1 Corinthians 4:5

DAY 38

> For examples of patience in suffering, dear brothers and sisters, look at the prophets who spoke in the name of the Lord. We give great honor to those who endure under suffering. For instance, you know about Job, a man of great endurance. You can see how the Lord was kind to him at the end, for the Lord is full of tenderness and mercy. *James 5:10–11*

In my counseling practice, when I listen to someone anxiously pour out his personal concern and fear over something he's dealing with, it's always great to see the sense of relief that floods over his face when he finds out that his feelings are normal, and that others face the same challenges and have the same concerns. It just makes us feel better to know that others have gone through what we have to go through.

James gives that kind of encouragement in today's verses. In yesterday's reading, James urged his readers to be patient, but he knows they need more encouragement. He points to all the prophets who patiently endured some difficult situations. And then he points them to the one person in the faith that was renowned for his patience—Job. Job suffered tremendous, tremendous loss and yet look at how it all ended up for him! Be encouraged by this guy, James encourages us.

Now, it's important to note that Job didn't just passively sit by while trouble came upon him from every side. If you carefully read the book of Job, you sense Job was anything but patient. He passionately questions and even resents what happens to him, and struggles to deal with his so-called friends who want Job to help them understand what's up with God in all this. James described Job as having *hupomone*, the Greek word for a patient endurance, not a passive patience. It's a resiliency of spirit that can take it all on and come out with an even stronger faith on the other side.[1] The rest of Job's story affirms this truth, as God eventually blessed Job with even more than he had before the test, and Job was able to see how God used his troubles for good, in Job's life and in the lives of others.

Draw strength and courage from Job, James says. Look at what God did in the end. And then James summed it all up: The Lord is full of tenderness and mercy. That's the kind of God who asks us to do what He says, and He can be trusted to do what's best for us.

———————— **So what?** ————————

1.   What makes you question your faith in God right now?

2. Where can you see from your friends' experiences that God is full of tenderness and mercy, and will you draw strength from them?

────────── **Prayer** ──────────

God, forgive my impatience. May I grow to be like Job, that my questions and doubts serve to grow my faith even stronger still. Thank You, Lord, for your great tenderness and mercy to me. Amen.

────── **More words from the Word** ──────

Job 42:10–12
Psalm 94:12
Matthew 5:12
Matthew 24:13

DAY 39

Some people like to find loopholes, and they're really good at it. They're called lawyers. Calm down, I'm just kidding. Really. Loopholes sometimes happen because no one could foresee the situation that created the unclear area. But then there are those who try to deceive another by disguising or hiding a loophole. They're called teenagers. Okay, okay, I'll stop.

James is giving instruction about loopholes in this verse, and it's the same teaching Jesus gave in the Sermon on the Mount found in the book of Matthew. In that day, people would bind an agreement with an oath, like we agree on a deal by "shaking on it." But the oath stuff had gotten way out of hand. If they used the name of God, the oath was binding; if they didn't, the deal wasn't sealed. But often, a person would try to trick the other into thinking the deal was binding, only to later say the agreement wasn't sealed. I imagine it would be like trying to mislead someone while playing "Simon

Says." When I was a kid, my friends would make fake promises like that. They would argue, "Hey, I didn't swear on the Bible, so it didn't count."

James, like Jesus, just says a simple, truthful "yes" or "no" will do. Quit trying to deceive people. Live honestly and let your word become trustworthy in the eyes of others. Speak the truth, and you will become known as one who can be trusted to keep your word. Stop playing semantics, and quit trying to find loopholes. And if you do happen to find one, don't exploit it—that's just wrong. So, no more half-truths and disguised lies; just tell the truth.

—————— **So what?** ——————

1. When you discover an undefined loophole, do you pride myself for being a shrewd businessperson?

2. Do you need to go and make amends with someone for taking advantage of them?

3. Is your word known to be honest?

—————— **Prayer** ——————

God, continue to show me the right and honest thing to do. I pray that my word will become and remain trustworthy among those who know me well. Amen.

—— More words from the Word ——

Matthew 5:34–37
Matthew 23:16–22

DAY 40

> Are any of you suffering hardships? You should pray. Are any of you happy? You should sing praises. Are any of you sick? You should call for the elders of the church to come and pray over you, anointing you with oil in the name of the Lord. Such a prayer offered in faith will heal the sick, and the Lord will make you well. And if you have committed any sins, you will be forgiven.
>
> *James 5:13–15*

When I was a senior in college my dad died from a brain tumor. He was sick for seventeen months. I remember praying the most fervent prayers I knew how to pray for his healing. My dad was a believer, but I wanted him to be around for a lot longer. I still don't know why God didn't heal him, but I know God has healed others. I see in the Gospels that Jesus didn't heal every sick person that he saw. The truth is God didn't promise to heal our bodies, and every physical healing is just a temporary miracle anyway. But Jesus did heal all who came to him with spiritual needs, and I saw the evidence in my dad's life that he received that kind of healing as well.

The word for "sick" that James uses is the Greek word *asthenei*, and it literally means "to be weak." In the Gospels of Matthew, Mark, Luke and John, this word is used for physical needs. In the book of Acts and in the Letters, it's used for spiritual weaknesses and needs. Surely God heals people of physical suffering, then and now. But as James has been teaching about patient endurance, he focuses on those who have grown weary, morally and spiritually, under the strain. For those who are hurting and sick from your spiritual battles, come to the leaders of the church for help. Let them pray over you, refresh your spirit with their prayers and anointing with oil, and let God do His good work in you. When we anoint people with oil in our churches, we do so as a sign of encouragement, not as a magic potion. God does the work of healing, not the oil, or the oil-er or the oil-ee. He does work through the strength of our faithful prayers, and by the power of His name, sins are forgiven. Prayer heals. Prayer encourages and builds up.

And that's a reason to be thankful and sing praises to our great God!

———————— **So what?** ————————

1. Do you need refreshment for a weary soul?

2. What can you give God thanks for that will help lift your spirit and renew you?

3. Ask someone to pray with you. God's power is magnified through their faithful prayers joined with yours!

———————— **Prayer** ————————

God, You are so great. Thank You for all Your blessings. Lift my spirit as I pray for my weariness. . . . Amen.

—— **More words from the Word** ——

Psalm 50:14,15
Isaiah 33:24
Mark 6:13

DAY 41

> Confess your sins to each other and pray for each other so that you may be healed. The earnest prayer of a righteous person has great power and produces wonderful results.
>
> *James 5:16*

E verybody believes that prayer works. It's just that it sometimes takes a hurricane or a terrorist attack to motivate some people to pray. When the going gets really tough, you'll be hard-pressed to find somebody who's not praying, even if they haven't prayed in months or years. Some people pray as a last resort instead of a first resource.

James says to pray as a first resort. There's no reason not to, and every reason to do so. The brother of Jesus goes on to say the fervent prayer of a righteous person has great power. But, if you want to pull the plug out of the power of prayer, then just dishonor God in some area of your life on a continual basis. Your prayers just won't work. If you're harboring resentment and unforgiveness in your heart, for instance, God says you'll need to clear that up first.

That's why James says that confession and reconciliation are vital. When we humble (there's that word again) ourselves to ask forgiveness from another person, it clears up the prayer channel with our Father again. And there are other really great benefits as well. James says to pray for each other; it's hard to stay mad at someone you pray for. And forgiveness is wonderful for our mental and spiritual fitness. "If physical exercise had a mental equivalent, it would probably be the process of forgiveness."[1]

When we do what we need to do to have our heart right with God and then pray, James says *Watch out*. The power and results are *incredible*. We need to remember God does not grant any requests we make that would hurt us or others or that would violate His own nature or will. For our prayers to be fulfilled, our requests must be in harmony with the principles of God's Kingdom. The stronger our belief, the more likely our prayers will be in line with God's will, and then God will be happy to grant them.

So pray believing as much as you can!

 **So what?**

1. Is there some unresolved issue you have with someone that's jamming your communication with God?

2. How can you best pray for your enemies and other difficult people in your life?

3. Pray for God's exponential power!

―――――――――― **Prayer** ――――――――――

God, soften my heart to move me to ask forgiveness from those I've offended. Expand my understanding of Your power so I pray with more expectancy, and I'll be a larger part of what You are doing in Your world. Amen.

―――― **More words from the Word** ――――

Numbers 11:2
Matthew 18:15–18
Matthew 21:22
Mark 9:21–24

DAY 42

Elijah was as human as we are, and yet when he prayed earnestly that no rain would fall, none fell for three and a half years! Then, when he prayed again, the sky sent down rain and the earth began to yield its crops. *James 5:17–18*

Just like James did when he used Job as an encouraging example to those who need encouragement in patient endurance, He points to another great person of faith who knew the power of prayer: the famous prophet Elijah.

Elijah had a tough job. He had to deliver a message to King Ahab, who wasn't going to like it before he even heard it, just because Elijah was the messenger. They had some history. Elijah was a loner who was very connected with God nonetheless.

Elijah told the king there was to be no dew or rain after he spoke the word, and it happened just as he said. This was God's call to repentance for all the evil people in the land. Then Elijah took on all 450 of Queen Jezebel's prized Baal prophets (the king's chosen religion) in a challenge to show whose God was all-powerful. After God's incredible display of fire from heaven at Elijah's word,

Elijah won the people over and had all of the prophets killed.

After that victory, Elijah went up to the top of a mountain and prayed fervently for rain. After the seventh prayer, Elijah's servant saw a very small cloud forming out of the sea. Soon the sky became black with clouds and wind . . . and heavy rain.

The fervent prayer of *any* righteous person will have powerful and great results. Elijah was just as human as you and me. But that prayer power can only be tapped when we have that authentic relationship with God like Elijah did.

As a pastor, there are many times when someone will ask me to pray for them because I have a "direct line upstairs." My answer is always the same: "I'll certainly pray for you, but your prayers are just as effective as mine." I'm so glad I serve a God like that!

———————— So what? ————————

1.   Have you sold myself short in recognizing the power of your prayers?

2.   What can you pray for today, expecting great results?

——————— **Prayer** ———————

God, I pray that I will want to keep my relationship with You growing and more intimate each day. Lord, show me where You are answering my prayers. Amen.

—— **More words from the Word** ——

1 Kings 17:1
1 Kings 18:41–46

DAY 43

My dear brothers and sisters, if someone among you wanders away from the truth and is brought back, you can be sure that whoever brings the sinner back will save that person from death and bring about the forgiveness of many sins. *James 5:19–20*

What would be your reaction if you saw a billboard or Twitter post that read: "Does God want you to marry a prostitute? Come to First Non-Denominational Church this Sunday and find out!" Believe it or not, that was the prophet Hosea's lot in life. God told him to marry Gomer, the town prostitute. So he did. Wow. They had children, but Gomer wandered back to her former ways, and Hosea humbled himself as he went out looking for his lover in the streets of his town. When he found her, he *bought* her back for about the price he would pay for a servant, to once again claim her as his own.

It's a different kind of love story, to be sure. But this story tells of that same kind of love that God has for his people. He wants us for His own, keeps pursuing after us, even when we leave Him, and when we return, He teaches us again the depths of what real love is.

Greg Griffin

When Jesus walked the earth, he told great stories of a lost sheep being sought after and found, and a son who returned home to a loving Father after a prideful departure. These stories also illuminated the love God has for us His children.

And then, James says a similar thing as he closes his letter in tenderness. Just as God seeks after us when we wander, we need to go seek after a brother or sister who has wandered. And there is a great blessing in the process, for both the wanderer and the retriever.

James shows us an important truth. One *can* wander away.[1] And the word he chose for the wanderer lets us know this isn't the woman or man who has missed a couple of fellowship dinners. Their life is *way* off track spiritually. James gives encouragement to those who take on the mission of restoration. The rich reward for returning one who was lost back to the fold of God snatches them from the jaws of spiritual death, and connects you with the God you serve in an even deeper and more profound way.

That is nothing less than sharing the loving works of a relentlessly loving God. Sure, it's risky — and it's worth the risk. The reward is great. So, go. Just do it.

───────── **So what?** ─────────

1. What is the value of one soul to God?

2.   Who do you have a relationship with that God may be asking you to go look for and invite back to the Body of Christ?

 Prayer

God, let the incomprehensible depth of Your love for me move me to be an agent of that kind of love for people who need it most. Amen.

More words from the Word

Proverbs 10:12
Hosea 1:2–3
Luke 15
Romans 11:14
1 Corinthians 1:21

Vital Faith

——————— Now what? ———————

Now that you've finished this study, I hope you'll meditate on the above question: *Now what?* If you're task-oriented like me, it would be easy to check the box and put this book on the shelf. My prayer is that some truths or Scriptures from this study have some staying power — they've moved into long-term memory and you can call upon their strength when you need it in the days ahead.

Here are a few encouragements to carry on from here with what God has impressed upon you from His Word.

Reread James once a month for the next three months. It's only five chapters and how long can that take, you know? Set a reminder on your device . . . do it now.

Make note cards of the Scriptures that you want to hold on to the most. Stick one by the bathroom mirror. Put one by your computer. Put one on the family note board in the kitchen, or on the refrigerator. You get the idea. Repetition works.

If you've done this study in a group, consider staying together and diving in on a different study. Google "Bible study" and you're there.

Plan on rereading the study in one year to compare how much you may have retained, lost or learned in that time. Set a reminder . . . .

These are just a few thoughts to encourage you in your walk with Jesus. The health and vitality of that one relationship will alter the trajectory of the rest of your life, and affect the lives of those around you.

So, as James might say to us, "Just do it."

Notes

Day 1

1. William Barclay, *The Letters of James and Peter* (Philadelphia: Westminster, 1976), p. 35.

Day 4

1. Robert Beers et al., eds., *Life Application Study Bible* (Wheaton, IL: Tyndale House, 1996), p. 1985.

Day 5

1. Stephen Covey, *The Seven Habits of Highly Effective Families* (New York: Golden Books, 1997), p. 22.

Day 8

1. Stephen Covey, *The Seven Habits of Highly Effective People* (New York: Simon & Schuster, 2004), p. 235.

Day 9

1. Barclay, *Letters of James and Peter*, p. 57.

Day 18

1.   Beers, *Life Application Study Bible*, p. 1985.

Day 21

1.   Albert Harper et al., eds., *The Wesley Study Bible* (Nashville: Thomas Nelson, 1990), p. 1869.

Day 23

1.   Beers, *Life Application Study Bible*, p. 1988.

Day 25

1.   John Bunyan, *The Pilgrim's Progress* (New York: P.F. Collier & Son, 1909), p. 16.

Day 26

1.   Dave Moreland, "All That Was Missing Was a Flashing 'Arrest Me' Sign," *Dave Moreland's Bozo Criminal of the Day*, June 21, 2016, http://www.electricferret.com/bozo/archive/14258-all-that-was-missing-was-a-flashing-arrest-me-sign/.

Day 27

1.   J.I. Packer, *Knowing God* (Downer's Grove, IL: Intervarsity, 1993), p. 80.

Day 30

1.   Barclay, *Letters of James and Peter*, p. 102.

Day 31

1.   Barclay, *Letters of James and Peter*, p. 105.

Day 35

1.   "The Voice of the Martyrs," accessed August 31, 2016, http://www.persecution.com.

2.   DC Talk, *Jesus Freaks* (Bloomington, MN: Bethany House, 1999), p. 8.

Day 36

1.   Sir Fred Catherwood, *Evangelicals Now*, September 1994, front page.

Day 38

1.   Barclay, *Letters of James and Peter*, p. 125.

Day 41

1.   Brenda Goodman, "Forgiveness is Good, Up to a Point," *Psychology Today*, January 1, 2004, accessed August 31, 2016, https://www.psychologytoday.com/articles/200401/forgiveness-is-good-point.

Day 43

1.   Barclay, *Letters of James and Peter*, p. 133.

About the Author

Greg Griffin grew up in Virginia, and did all of his formal schooling there. He went to Randolph-Macon College and graduated with a BA double major in Religious Studies and Psychology. He went on to complete his MA in Christian Education at the Presbyterian School of Christian Education in Richmond. Greg worked for over 20 years as a youth pastor in three churches, and then as a lead pastor and church planter. He is now a Board Certified Pastoral Counselor and ordained Christian pastor in private practice in the Atlanta area, and the author of *Dungeon Times Survival Guide*. His passion is helping people find hope in life and healing in relationships.

He calls himself a "pastorpreneur" because he's a pastoral counselor, nonprofit executive/family advocate, fundraising company co-founder, teacher, and inventor, all at the same time. Really.

He enjoys family times with his two teenage sons, playing with his beagle/Jack Russell mix named Griffin (yeah, his name is Griffin Griffin), sports, exercise, and techno gadgets. He watches sports (especially the Redskins, Ohio State football, the Dodgers, and University of Virginia lacrosse), all things Marvel and DC Comics, Survivor, clean comedy on YouTube, and not much else.

Made in the USA
Charleston, SC
03 February 2017